THE FASHION
HUSTLE

WRITTEN BY: KING CEDRIC

CHAPTERS

CHAPTER 1
FAME OR FORTUNE

In the beginning you have to ask yourself, do you want to be rich or do you want to be famous? It's not enough that people know your name. Being a media darling will only get you so far. In order to be successful, you should think of yourself as a CEO first, fashion entrepreneur second.

A CEO is a manager of people, finances, and processes. Therefore, you will have a great deal of responsibility and important business decisions will face you each and every day. The buck stops with you and the business should always be at the forefront of your mind, not just an afterthought.

One of the first decisions to make when you come up with a business idea is whether to do it alone or with a partner. You have probably heard that entering into a partnership with your company is like entering into a marriage, and it is true. Partnerships like marriages are exciting because the whole is greater than the individual parts and together amazing offspring can be born. Like marriages partnerships require work, the ability to compromise, and they have real cost. Decision-making and control is shared; equity and wealth potential is diluted.

So just like getting hitched on a whim in Vegas is not necessarily a great long term idea, you shouldn't pick a partner unless you think you need to. And if you do need to, make sure that person is a hard worker and focused. Often it is a spouse (Patrizio Bertelli is married to Miuccia Prada), sibling (Christopher Kane's sister Tammy runs the business) or a friend (Marc Jacobs has long time business partner Robert Duffy) who might take on this role. With a partner not only do you have someone to lean on in times of difficulty, you also have a division of roles, which allows you to focus more on the creative aspects of the business. The three examples below, will give you more insight on the importance of entering into balanced paternership.

🖤*EXAMPLE I (HUSBAND & WIFE) : Fashion legend Miuccia Prada of Prada and Miu Miu has been on the style radar for best-dressed awards, as well as sensational designs of nylon backpacks, motif pleated skirts and thick wedge shoes. Since taking over the family-owned luxury goods company in 1978, Miuccia has always been in the front row of growing the brand with husband and business partner Patrizio Bertelli. Having first met at a trade fair in Milan in 1977, Miuccia hired Patrizio as one of Prada's main handbag suppliers. Eight years later, they got married and the rest is history. While Miuccia is the lead designer, Patrizio handles the business and label most would associate with his wife. Yet with working together comes the occasional friction and the couple is known for their violent arguments. Miuccia once shared, "We work hard. It's always an intense relationship, and it's exhausting having to work with him. But I admire and respect him." With Miuccia as one of the most influential designers in the world and Patrizio as the motivational influence behind her, this stylish power couple has a combined worth of billions. An industry insider once said that "Miuccia's creativity and Bertelli's management make them a successful fashion couple.*

*❦ EXAMPLE II (BROTHER & SISTER) : Christopher Kane...
how the designer's sister made him a global brand....
If he was a star before, he is a supernova now, along with his sister and business partner Tammy, who is the energy at the core of the growing Kane Empire. So much so in fact that Vogue's fashion features director Sarah Harris suggests that, if Tammy would allow it, "Christopher would have her out on the runway with him to accept applause".*

But in a modest email to the Standard, Tammy played down her invaluable role in Kane's success story. "Mainly I manage the business and share an office with Christopher so we are always together. Christopher draws up ideas for the collections and I help him edit those ideas." By his big sister's account — "we protect each other" she says — Christopher Kane is an "extraordinary creative talent" who is set to benefit from the creative independence the deal with PPR has promised to provide.

*Born near Motherwell, five years before her baby brother, Tammy has long been Christopher's number one fan. As children the two were inseparable and hid out in one another's bedrooms after nightmares. As teens they shopped together in Glasgow city center with Christopher advising Tammy on her Saturday night outfit choices.
Having decided on a career in fashion at an early age, Tammy completed a degree at the prestigious Scottish College of Textile Design before making a move to London in 2002 at the same time as Christopher, who had enrolled at Central Saint Martins to do a fashion degree of his own. He launched his eponymous label immediately after graduation.*

Ten years on, Tammy, described by Harris as Christopher's "muse, model, manager and sounding Wboard", is at the heart of the Kane brand.

"It was Tammy who inspired his career in the first place," says Susannah Frankel, fashion director at Grazia.

Despite being something of an icon for the British fashion industry, Tammy — recognizable by her striking blue eyes and jet black hair — who appeared in Love Magazine last September alongside her newborn baby Bonnie. But she is the strong silent partner. And theirs is a unique, collaborative process.

For Natalie Kingham, the senior womenswear buyer at Matches and long-term follower of the Kane brand, it is Tammy's astute ability to understand what women want to wear that makes her Christopher's secret weapon. "Christopher creates the clothes and Tammy test runs them," says Kingham. "While she is incredibly talented and beautiful, she is a regular woman saying this works for me. She is neither untouchable nor unreachable. That's a great thing to have." Harris is equally convinced. "Tammy is the brand," she says. "I remember his first show. Every model had long hair, center parted — they were like mini Tammy's striding out. Christopher designs with her in mind. Its second nature to him — since an early age, he's always made and bought clothes for her to wear, and I think if she said she wouldn't wear something, then he wouldn't put it out on the catwalk."

As a result, when it came to signing on the dotting line with PPR, the role of his sister is undoubtedly one that ranked high on Christopher's agenda. "The business support network around us is to free me up to focus on the elements of the job I love the best and am best at," says Tammy, "helping Christopher realize his ideas."
It's been a seamless 30-year working relationship so far.
Courtesy of standard.co.uk

EXAMPLE III (FRIENDS) JACOBS ON DUFFY:

Robert was working for a company called Reuben Thomas, and they were looking to start a contemporary sportswear division. After he saw my work at Parsons, he approached me. He gave me a chance without my having any experience whatsoever to design full-time. Since then, Robert has been the biggest believer in terms of my creative vision, and I guess I am towards his. It's really important for me to have his validation and his belief. It's not that I lack confidence in my creative team, but I always like to have that moment when I'm sitting with Robert and I explain what we're doing and get his feedback. Even if he's not 100 percent sure, it's important for me to know that he knows. It's about the relationship, that started when there was nobody else—just Robert and me.

Sometimes we disagree on creative situations. He'll look at me like I'm out of my mind, like when I wanted to play "Somewhere over the Rainbow" for last fall's show. He said, "You're not really going to use that?" And then he sort of said, "All right." He's never stopped me from doing something. Sometimes we see each other constantly and sometimes there are weeks or maybe even a month where we don't speak. We don't micromanage each other.

I think that some of Robert's great successes, like BookMarc [a bookstore on Bleecker Street] and his real-estate decisions, are born of passion and instinct, not with a calculator. When he decided to open the shops in the West Village or on Mercer Street just before the Mercer [hotel] opened, he had a personal attachment to those neighborhoods but also an instinctive sense that they would become a destination.

Ultimately I don't have any crystal ball either in terms of designing a bag or a shoe or a collection, but at some point, even with my own sense of insecurity, I just let go and think, "Well, this is what I feel we should be doing for the next season, so we're going to do it," and we just kind of go for it. That's a quality that Robert and I share.

His stresses, like mine, are greater and greater. There are more stores and more employees. He has to make more trips, opening stores for us, and be away from home so often. Then he's got to be the cheerleader at Vuitton and listen when I brief him on what we're doing there. It doesn't mean there are more hours in the day, but he still manages to find the time to be there, to help, to be a good leader.

On a personal level, Robert probably cares about me more than anyone in my entire life—about my well-being as well as my ability to perform as a designer. He literally saved my life. As soon as he realized [my heroin addiction in 1999] he said, "I'm not going to sit back and watch you kill yourself." He took the bull by the horns and went to Mr. Arnault [CEO of LVMH] and said, "Marc needs to get help." He did a press release.

He called Bridget Foley at Women's Wear Daily to do a story. He and I philosophically agreed that it was not about hiding a problem. I've never avoided any kind of discussion about my personal life or rehab. I could probably afford to be that way because I have Robert's support.

I can see why people want to compare us to other fashion partnerships, but our relationship is a bit different. We've never been lovers, like Bergé and Saint Laurent and Giammetti and Valentino, although people always thought we were. But it's a difficult job, both sides of this job.

That's why I say it's not about what I do and what Robert does. The two of us together are Marc Jacobs. The two of us together are Vuitton. I don't think without him or without me we could achieve all that we've achieved.

Courtesy of WSJ.com —Edited from Mistry's interviews with Duffy and Jacobs

As you see partnerships managed correctly can create amazing brands. Solo entrepreneurs can also, realize successful brands with a strong team. You have to always remember the fashion industry is a business and its ruthlessness requires honesty, organization, and vision. I think the business of fashion gets overlooked in many fashion schools and many fashion professionals in the industry are not well-rounded enough. For example, if you are studying to be a designer you should take classes on production, marketing, and business. There are great designers who do not know how things are produced and many of them have been working as designers for years. Remember, fashion is a business of nickels and dimes and you must always ask yourself "How frugal can I be?" and "How am I going to finance this business?"

Use all your resources in the beginning to finance your business:

- *beg and borrow*
- *sell unnecessary things you own*
- *look for grant money*
- *get a loan*
- *sell equity in the company (Venture Capitalist)*
- *use crowd-funding platforms like kickstarter.com*
- *have private clients*
- *DON'T quit your day job (just yet).*

Don't spend your money on things like tradeshows and fashion shows until you can sell to a retailer. Before you do anything, always think about the ROI (return on investment). In business, there is a reason we often hear about conventional wisdom. There can be great pressure to do things the way things have always been done. But is conventional wisdom always correct? Trial and error has taught business leaders, often painfully, to steer towards an established set of norms and processes because history has shown that these practices increase the likelihood of success. If you are already selling a product, you should have excellent access to valuable sales data. Use it. Read the reports generated by your store or website and ask your accounts for sales summaries. The information is generally available, you just have to ask for it.

Important metrics to focus on are:
- *unit sales*
- *total volume*
- *sell through percent*
- *net gross margin*
- *net average retail price and returns*

After analyzing the metrics, keep in mind sell-through is only a function of the success a product achieves related to how you or your buyers purchased it. So, while this is an important measure, it can exclude some important contextual information that should always be considered as well. A good buy from the same collection can significantly lift sell-through. A tangible lack of data and facts, plus the collapse of seasonal fashion is putting a lot of pressure on the way the industry works today. Most businesses have sales reporting or business intelligence to know what is selling, so you should already understand the value of data at a trading level.

This sales data combined with a great understanding of your customer, inspiration from trend services or your own research is what you can use to make an educated guess about where things are going. But even the geniuses can't get it 100 percent right — otherwise clearance sales wouldn't exist because everything would sell through!

Seasonal fashion is dead and speed-to-market now is the market — even on the high end. Many brands that work with me are doing 8 or more drops a year, so although the weather is seasonal, fashion is constantly variable. People expect to see new garments on every visit to a store and the production capacity is there to make it happen. Traditional forecasting isn't a good fit when production can be so close to the market. The cleverest businesses can know exactly what their customers want by using technology. You can measure consumers and the entire trading environment. Customers express themselves constantly online either through Twitter, IG, Snapchat, on their blog, clicking a 'Like' button, adding a product to a basket, or buying something. The retail market is measurable — there's never been more accurate, factual information on exactly what's happening in real-time than now. It's an incredible strategic advantage.

Now that you are in the market you have to ask yourself "Are We Operating the Business at Scale?" Operating the business at scale means allocating and optimizing resources to drive the greatest results and volume across market-segment. Are marketing and sales working together to generate demand and close business? Are closed deals being transitioned to services/support to be nurtured? Are partners being leveraged to multiply the company's marketing, sales and services efforts to reach new customers and displace the competition? Operating the business at scale is about optimization, not duplication, of efforts.

I have seen brands leverage their size by negotiating exclusive dealings, favorable terms and volume discounts with other retail or manufacturing partners. Partnering with large businesses can also provide you with access to national and worldwide markets to sell products and services. In addition, keeping costs low or unchanged while increasing sales volume provides you with the opportunity to further decrease prices – gain new customers, more market-share – without sacrificing margin (economies of scale).

During a calendar/fiscal year the fashion industry has periods where we experience increased customer demand for products and services (e.g., during the holiday season). Core infrastructure offerings from organizations like Amazon Web Services enable retailers to increase server capacity (scale-up) when customer demand is high without having to invest in new hardware. Retailers can then reduce server capacity (scale-down) during normal operating periods. These types of offerings/products allow you to pay for what you need, when you need it. Companies that scale have operating leverage. They can grow revenue with minimal or no increase in operating costs (e.g., administrative, sales, etc.).

Example to illustrate Scale:

♘   *In Year 1, company delivers $10M in revenue with $1M in operating costs. In Year 2, company delivers $12M in revenue with $1M in operating costs. Company scales because it grew revenue by $2M without increasing its operating costs.*

♘   *In contrast, if company's operating costs increase by the same amount as its revenue, the business does not scale. That is, if company requires its operating costs to increase by $2M in order to grow its revenue by $2M, the business is not scaling.*

One way you can scale is through channel partners. Brands multiply their marketing, sales and services efforts with partner resources in exchange for a percentage of the margin. For example, if a brand has ten direct sellers, it is limited by the reach of those ten sellers. However, if the brand partners with a reseller with 50 sellers, the brand has increased its sales force (in theory) by 500%. Sharing 30% of the margin is less expensive than the cost of hiring an additional 50 sellers. Brands also use marketing to scale the business. Marketing enables Brands to effectively (results) and efficiently (cost and speed) communicate to customers with the right message at the right time. Marketing also helps generate customer demand and drive pipeline velocity for sales, which reduces selling costs. Driving customers and prospects to one-to-many events (e.g., product launches etc.) is a common way to scale with marketing. Last, but not least once a brand has developed a repeatable sales model, the next logical step is to invest in headcount to accelerate (and scale) the business. In fashion, this means adding sellers/territories within geographies to localize the business. For example, if the brand has developed a successful, repeated sales model in Seattle, WA, it can grow (scale) revenue by implementing the same sales model in San Francisco, CA. In the retail industry, it is the same theory for opening new stores.

How you answer the question "Am I in this for Fame or Fortune?" – is going to be the key to your success.

Notes:

CHAPTER 2
WORK BACKWARDS

Starting any new business that requires manufacturing, such as a clothing brand, can be capital intensive, and the thought of trying to pursue this venture without any funding can be extremely daunting, therefore you should consider working backwards. Start by asking yourself what your product is worth in the mind of the consumers. The consumer does not care how much it costs you to make the garments. Most of them will not know the difference between the various textiles, such as viscose, silk, satin, etc. They only care about what it cost to purchase it. Limit your risk by limiting the amount of fabrics you use in your collections and do not be afraid of minimums or MOQ (Minimum Order Quantity).

📖 *MOQ specifies the lowest quantity of a certain product that a supplier is willing to sell. The MOQ requirement cannot simply be negotiated away or vanish.*

While some suppliers may accept a slightly lowered MOQ, requesting it to be removed completely is the same as asking your supplier to lose money for the sake of your business. Many importers try to play the "my orders will be larger in the future" card, but suppliers hear this on an almost daily basis and only a fraction of their buyers can back up the claim in the end.

However, there are ways you can satisfy the supplier as well as order a smaller quantity:

- *Reuse components, materials, and colors on several products. This way the supplier can limit the number of subcontractors involved.*

- *Coordinate your orders with other designers; if you have friends or associates that you know who are developing collections using the same fabrications coordinate your production with them.*

- *Make sure that you are designing and developing a product that can reasonably be produced. While that may sound like an obvious point, many talented designers create beautiful concepts that prove to be too expensive or complicated to produce at scale.*

Always be sure that every detail of the product is truly creating value for a customer. With a retail markup, of 6 times production cost, every dollar you are adding to the cost of producing a garment will add around $6 to the final retail price. Your products should have clear target cost, derived from working backward from final retail pricing.

Make sure to build in a realistic margin for yourself that considers not only the pure costs of production, but also other monies that you will have to spend in order to get the product into a selling environment. This includes things like:

- *Duties*
- *Freight*
- *Fees*
- *Commissions*
- *Warehousing*
- *Sampling*
- *Development costs*

Keep in mind that samples are often one of the single biggest line items in the design process and can swing a seemingly profitable collection into the red. Ask yourself, what is the one business goal that you want to achieve with your first run? Do you want to brand yourself for your every-season basics? Do you want to establish what pieces are your best repeat buys or sell-through the whole collection? If you cannot define the most important goal of your first run, production should be held off. Being able to communicate your main goal with a manufacturer may even allow them to extend their services beyond just production, and give you invaluable help in achieving your goals.

Although samples are the biggest line item as far as cost, they are the heart of apparel production. They make up the collection, lead to the perfect fit, instruct production, and act as the showpieces that bring in business. Arguably, they are the most essential part of apparel production. But how do you go about making one, what are the types of samples, and how exactly are they utilized?

The first sample is your prototype. To successfully create a great prototype, follow these 5 steps:

❦   *Determine the size of your samples.*

Ask yourself what the samples will be used for. Possibly as a sales tool, for photo shoots, or a runway show is usually the first response. But they also will most likely be used for your first fitting, which means that you will want your sample to be a size that can be logically graded both up and down to achieve a good fit in all your desired sizes.

❦   *Understand your sample size's body measurements.*

These measurements are not necessarily the same as your clothing specs, but knowing the body measurement underneath your designs will give you a better idea of what your clothing measurement should be. It is also important to understand that not all size 6 garments fit the same way, so understanding your brand's definition of that size is important to your brand identity as well.

❦   *Create a flat sketch.*

This is also known as a technical drawing or just simply, a flat. A good flat sketch has simple lines, with no shading or coloring in, and can be done by hand or with Adobe Illustrator. It is important to have a clear outline of your silhouette as if it were lying flat. You can then add a solid line at any place where there is a seam, and represent all stitching with dashed lines, zigzags or other renderings of specific stitches. Pattern makers use these renderings to create the patterns, so simple lines rather than stylized are always best.

❧ *Give initial specs.*

Specs are the measurements of a garment laid out in an easy to read chart. For the most part, a patternmaker will need the basic specs such as body length, sweep circumference, across shoulder, sleeve length, etc. This is when knowing your sample size body measurements will come in handy. Be sure to note any placements of trims or embellishments. It is also helpful to understand your fabric and how the stretch, thickness and drape will affect your garment and therefore your measurements.

❧ *Organize all your fabric and trims*

To avoid mistakes, it is essential to provide your sample room with all the supplies needed for your garment in an organized and easy to follow way.

Many times, the first thing done with a sample is a fitting to determine what fit or style changes need to happen to the pattern in order to perfect the style. It is a good idea to get this process done early as it can mean resampling and can sometimes take more than one round of revisions.

Once your pattern corrections have been made, it is time to make your sales samples (also known as duplicate samples) in the colors you choose for marketing and sales. Ideally, sales samples consist of one piece in each color in the sample size. Since sales figures often are largest for the colors the sales rep has on hand, it is often decided to invest in a full set to sell. Sales samples are commonly used for photo shoots and runway shows. However, if the designer opted for sales samples in an alternate size for the sake of proper fit or to better suit a particular target customer, it is possible the patterns will need to be graded prior to photo shoot samples being made.

The final sample needed is your production sew-by sample. This, along with your tech-pack, is what your production team will use as a guide. Generally, designers give a factory a sew-by sample and all supplies needed to create a garment, then ask for a prototype to be made for approval. Once the approval is given, and the bulk supplies are delivered, the factory uses their garment as the standard for producing the larger order. With all these samples and everything else that goes on in the meantime, it is easy to get confused about which sample is which! So, for the sake of organization, it is a good idea to create a sample card with your name/logo and general information about the specific garment.

❖ Costing Formula

A simple formula for calculating the cost of a single garment is to add the cost of the fabric, trims and notions, labor and overhead. The result, along with the desired profit percentage, can be used to set the garment's retail price. For a small-business owner who doesn't mass-produce items, the margin and mark-up is generally higher than it is for larger businesses that produce in quantity due to differences in volume.

❖ Determining Production Overhead

Many small-business owners set a standard fixed and variable expense allocation at the beginning of each year. To do this, first make annual sales projections relating to the number of garments the business expects to produce over the coming year. Next, add the total of all fixed expenses such as rent, property taxes and equipment depreciation. Finish by dividing total fixed expenses by the annual production projection.

For if example, if fixed expenses come to $75,000 and the business expects to produce 5,000 garments over the coming year, $15 will be allocated to each garment produced to cover fixed expense overhead. Do the same for variable expenses, using actual costs -- except for time -- from the previous year as a guide.

Defining a goal for production is important because not only will it shape the way you decide brand assortment (many pieces vs. limited editions, shallow vs. deep), going into production with a goal will help you stick to putting your efforts toward the most important things, rather than trying to do everything. Working with factories is not for wallflowers. You have to demand respect and stay on top of communicating with the factories to get the job done! Everything is negotiable. It is a game of back and forth communications to decide on a final price that works for both parties.

Notes:

CHAPTER 3
REAL LIFE COSTING

The biggest excuses people make are "I don't have any money" and "I don't have time." There is never a right time to start a business, some ideas are great but they are just too far ahead of their time and they fail. Some ideas are great but they arrive at the party too late and they fail. You just need to do it! Determine what it will cost you to start the business. A logo can cost you $75 or $1 million (the price some corporations spend on their logos). It's a business of nickels and dimes as I mentioned in Chapter 1. Spend your money wisely.

When starting your company, one of the most important decisions you will make are how and when your company grows. Growing a young company is not an involuntary, linear process, like how a baby grows. Growth tends to happen in sizeable, step-up increments, like a set of stairs, based upon deliberate decisions you and your team make. The key is to balance careful planning with speed of execution. Be prepared for "real life" costs that are not included in textbook costing.

Design with a cost sheet, if you're looking to make your line into a successful business you need to integrate the business side with the creative side. Consider the cost of every pattern piece and every stitch to ensure you stay within your market price point. Higher production costs will be added onto the final price tag, which will result in either losing sales or losing money—or both. Having an overview of the pieces in a collection and the number of samples you are going to make can make the difference between saving money and wasting money.

🖊 *Before you start clipping and cutting, sit down and plan your collection. Write down the number of dresses, tops, bottoms and the fabric you will use for each.*

This will not only help you start to visualize your collection, it will also help to ensure your collection is cohesive and works well together. Each item in your collection should complement each other - telling different parts of the same story.

Every successful fashion company rests upon the success of one or two items which form the foundation of the overall product assortment and a more predictable stream of revenue, around which a real business can be built. These products don't change dramatically from season to season and they become the staples of your product offering. For example; Tory Burch has her Reva Ballerina flats, Louis Vuitton has its leather goods and Andover & Hotchkiss has its Suits and Dress Shirts. Without this kind of solid foundation, it's difficult to build a successful business. In the middle are the products that you adapt and refresh each season with new colors, fabrics or prints, but the basic silhouettes remain the same. Over time, you may choose to slowly adapt these products and perfect them, but in general you are using tried and tested shapes which have already been proven in the market.

At the top of your collection are the purely seasonal elements which are more about driving interest and bringing new energy to your product mix. This may be the pieces you show on the runway and which are featured in editorial. From time to time, you may have a huge commercial hit at the top part of your collection, but as it's generally hard to predict exactly what will strike a chord (or which product your favorite A-list celebrity decides to wear), it can sometimes be hard for a small fashion business to capitalize on the short-term buzz generated by these types of products.

While fashion is a product business that often comes with exacting standards, it is still important to carefully manage your product development costs. Creating large, unfocused sample collections with very expensive fabrics can be a death knell for a young fashion company. Not only will you have spent a fortune on developing a set of samples, you may have also created a collection that could never sell at retail because it would be far too expensive. I think today a lot of consumers talk about wanting to be unique and having their personal style, but in actual fact, almost everyone belongs to one of a few sub-groups of style (Classic Americana, Soft Grunge, Modern Contemporary, Witch House, Health Goth, etc.) Since fashion went digital, everyone has access to the same information at the same time. And a lot is still very influenced by what goes on at the large luxury houses. Most shopping centers and main shopping streets have the same stores — many of them vertical retailers owned by multinational corporations who all have the same goal: to make money and expand. In order to do so, they have to look at what trends can be adapted for the mass market, which means the products are pretty much the same everywhere. The large groups, Kering and LVMH, operate according to the same formula.

In an industry where, for decades, unspoken gentleman's agreements relegated suppliers to silence and luxury brands kept their clandestine overseas production from the buying public, new notions of transparency are often hard to swallow. For many, particularly those at the higher-end, there is a sense that disclosing such information diminishes their competitive advantage or exposes them to predatory rivals. Companies always use this as an excuse - I don't think this argument holds water.

Mainstream attitudes toward transparency and traceability — defined as the disclosure of information relating to material sources, manufacturers and other suppliers in order for all stakeholders, including end consumers, to have a complete and accurate picture of the ethical and environmental impact of a product — have been changing as the fashion industry scrambles to catch up with rising customer expectations.

💮 *EXAMPLE I, Nike's Making app is an open-source tool for designers to become better informed about the environmental impact of the materials they use by scoring them based on properties such as chemical processes, energy and water consumption and greenhouse gas output. It can also be used as an ad-hoc guide for consumers to evaluate and compare Nike's products.*

💮 *EXAMPLE II, Nudie Jeans' interactive production guide digitally maps out the Swedish firm's global suppliers, subcontractors, and transportation information, while providing an audit summary and a portfolio of photographs of people at work and the facilities inside each factory. Nike's global manufacturing map covers similar ground and in some instances goes into even further detail. Not surprisingly, moves such as these have observers debating how much is good to share and when transparency becomes a liability.*

A well-resourced and determined competitor will always be able to discover a company's key suppliers. It is the responsible consumers, however, who don't have these resources and who are the ones needing reassurance. I'd say there's no evidence that transparency has ever harmed a business. Once the objectives, strategy and parameters have been clearly set surrounding a transparency initiative, getting the tone right can be just as important. Consumers are now more-savvy than ever before about a brands' target and investment in rapidly-growing corporate social responsibility departments. With this comes a heighted ability among shoppers for detecting whether transparency initiatives seem sincere or not. One way that fashion brands will ultimately be judged credible or not is by how they incorporate transparency into their commitment to social and environmental sustainability. In the case of Nudie, that credibility really began three years ago when it finally achieved its goal of becoming 100 percent organic which was set seven years earlier. Its new online production guide map appears to be just the first step in achieving its next goal of full transparency in the near future. I believe if you are proud of your brand, you will make sure we know about it. As you can see "Real Life Cost" can come in many form-- based on your brand strategy, how you want to position yourself in the marketplace, and if you want a scalable brand. Proper planning is the key..

Notes:

CHAPTER 4
STAY FOCUSED

Being focused is one of the most important things you can do to grow your business. Don't start a company unless there is nothing else in the world you want to do. Being the CEO of a start-up is all consuming. You no longer have weekends, holidays or carefree drinks after work. You are on constant alert, thinking about the people who work for you, planning out the future of your company, fussing over every small detail that might contribute to the success (or demise) of your business. The ups and downs are real and extreme. Warren Buffet, CEO of Berkshire Hathaway, once wrote: "No sooner is one problem solved than another surfaces—never is there just one cockroach in the kitchen." Mr. Buffet is right.

Life is a series of problems waiting to happen. Leaders, as point people in the management of people and ideas, encounter problems daily, even hourly. The successful ones learn to deal with them and develop techniques to manage and solve them. A leader must ask two questions when faced with a problem: What happens if we do nothing?

What happens if we do everything possible? Some problems cannot be solved no matter what you do; that problem calls for containment, or operational mode. Other problems need to be extinguished like fires—quickly, safely, and with maximum resources. Considering the outcomes narrows the options and provides a choice. Assess the situation...stand-back and take a deep breath.

Here are some ways to train your mind to think unconventionally when faced with problems:

- *Brainstorm. Get everyone together and throw out ideas. Be non-judgmental.*

- *Adopt the perspective of the customer: What would a customer want done to solve the problem?*

- *Dialogue. Get a trusted partner. Review the problem. Consider solutions.*

- *Create a visual metaphor. Create a pictogram of the problem. Present to others and discuss it.*

- *Think laterally. Look outside the problem to gain per pective. It involves awareness, alternatives, and provocation (i.e., stimulating creative thoughts.)*

- *Force Field Analysis. Draw two columns. Label one "forces for change." Label the other, "force against change." List forces for both columns. Discuss how to overcome the restraints so that positive change may occur.*

Another thing to consider as the leader of your company is how to keep yourself and team motivated.

You must display complete conviction and passion for what you are doing; anything short of that and your team will smell it, your partners will smell it, your customers will smell it and you will fail.

You must have the following:

❧   *Strict discipline*

❧   *An insane ability to be organized*

❧   *The ability to step back and see the big picture*

❧   *Thick skin*

❧   *Be a problem solver and not a problem dweller*

❧   *The gift of gab to be able to tell your story*

For example if you are starting a clothing brand, remember that your number one objective is to get the attention of the retail buyer. Do research by searching for topics on Facebook, Twitter and Instagram using #_____ (fill in the blank with the topic that relates to your business's subject matter or interests of your customers). Follow the people with the largest number of followers. Get to know them all the way down to the details, like the car they drive. Know your customer!

Figure out what makes your brand special to customers and make it a purchasing decision. For example, being eco-friendly is not only a purchasing decision, it's a value add. You must do your homework and design for your customer, not for yourself. If the design pleases your customers, they'll please you. If you insist on a design that only pleases you, your customers may not be inspired to buy your product or service and in the end you will lose.

Take your ego out of the equation!

The harsh reality is that regardless of how much money, time and sacrifice you put into your line, ninety-nine percent of the world still won't be swayed to pay attention to your work, which means that your work needs to be able to speak on its own. As fashion continues to be reshaped by digital media, 'differentiation' would seem to have the upper hand. 'Personal style,' 'beyond trend' and 'individual expression' are some of the catchphrases of our day as social media puts more power in the hands of individual consumers and, in theory, allows for the growth of more variety in tastes, styles and brands.

A successful brand will remain so as long as the leader and staff enhance its value in the eyes of the customers. When reviewing your brand, remember that your customers and employees have built up an emotional attachment to it and feel a sense of ownership in it. Your brand represents the whole customer experience, not just your signage or stationary. You should regularly review your customer and employee experiences, this will provide an early indication of any elements of your brand that are underperforming. Prompt action to correct any underperforming element can save a lot of money and negate the need to rebrand your whole business. Remember, your brand building is like storytelling. If done properly, you will not only appeal to your target customer, but make them want to put themselves right in the middle of the story.

When you are introducing a new brand into the market it can often times be seen as disruptive, and the fashion community will segregate into 5 different responses:

Fashion adaption life cycle

🖋 *Innovators (into the essence of fashion textile, protecting the old guard, purest, not interested in major success, couture designers)*

🖋 *Visionaries (true creativeness, wants retail to change constantly, rebels against every trend, introduce new shapes and silhouettes)*

🖋 *Pragmatists (want well-established references that your brand will be around, dislike risk. It connotes a "waste of money and time.)*

🖋 *Conservatives (waits to see if the new idea becomes a trend and shops primarily off mannequins)*

🖋 *Laggards (not into any new products and stuck in one style and not worth your time)*

The way to develop a fashion market is to work from top to bottom, focusing first on the innovators, growing that market, then moving on to the visionaries, growing that market, and so on... In this effort, companies must use each 'captured' group as a reference base for going on to market to the next group. Thus, the endorsement of innovators becomes an important tool for developing a credible pitch to the visionaries, that of the visionaries to the pragmatists, and so on.

There is a gap between the visionaries and pragmatists which I call "The Chasm". To cross the chasm, the goal is to create a pragmatist customer base that is referenceable, so they can provide us access to other mainstream prospects, since pragmatists use references in their buying decisions.

Getting beyond the chasm is extremely important. Pre-chasm commitments… are all too frequently simply unmaintainable in the [post-chasm period]. That is, they promise a level of performance or reward that, if delivered, would destroy the enterprise. This means that we'll need to manage our way out of the contradictions imposed by pre-chasm agreements. The first and best solution is to avoid making the wrong kind of commitments during the pre-chasm period. Your design concepts should provide a range from fashion basics to high fashion innovative designs. The purpose of the post-chasm enterprise is to make money. …We need to recognize that this is not the purpose of the pre-chasm organization." The purpose then, is to prove there is customer demand.

Crossing the chasm "involves a transformation in the enterprise… from being pioneers to becoming settlers." The people that helped you win the early market can now be a liability in the mainstream market.

> *To initiate the transition" from being pioneers to settlers, introduce these two new and temporary roles:*

Target Market Segment Manager

1. Transform a visionary customer relationship into a potential beachhead for entry into the mainstream vertical market of that customer.

2. Expedite the implementation of the first installation of the system.

3. During the implementation of the first installation, introduce into the account his own replacement, a true account manager.

4. Leverage the ongoing project to create one or more whole product extensions that solve some industry wide problem.

Whole Product Manager

1. This role's goal is to ultimately be a product marketing manager (in the marketing department, responsible for bringing the product to market). Manage the growing list of sales reports and product enhancements.

Always keep in mind the fashion business is a business, when you begin you have to determine the real cost of doing business. Which includes all processes to ensure you are creating a successful business. Reward the individuals that helped you get to each level of success to maintain high moral value and brand loyalty from within. For instance, pioneering salespeople should be rewarded immediately, for winning new accounts; settler account managers should be rewarded for longevity of the account, customer satisfaction, and predictability of revenue stream. Pioneering designers should be rewarded for early market penetration. Since early market returns are usually small, equity is used instead. However, cash should be used to reward settlers, not pioneers. At the end of the day, being an entrepreneur is not a profession, it is the output of a great idea. Know your idea, what the value proposition is and determine if you can win with it.

Notes:

CHAPTER 5
IT ALL STARTS WITH AN EMAIL

Network, Network, Network… It all starts with an email. Track how many people opened your email by using services like Mailchimp and Livehive. Follow up with the people that opened your email and visited your website. Sending a personal thank you note or offering a discount on the next purchase are both nice touches and good incentives for your customers to make future purchases.

Use your marketing, PR, and advertising budget to visit retailers. As a young designer, you probably don't need to spend money on advertising, and the expensive photo shoots and super slick branding that come along with it. You can still craft a very strong profile by building relationships with editors, journalists, photographers, and fashion insiders who take an interest in you and your work, and may help you for free.

These relationships will not only generate valuable editorial, their impact will also be felt longer than even the best-placed one-page ad in Vogue. As a young designer, you have a new and interesting story to tell and people will want to tell it too — you don't have to pay them for this privilege. Supplement this with a professional looking website that is in tune with your creative vision and has a clear brand identity that speaks to who you are creatively. Also, get the word out about your business by getting the editorial calendars for magazines from their websites and pitching them an idea for a story with your info—do this 3 months in advance.

There is nothing quite as valuable as a direct interaction with your customer. Reports may tell you what consumers bought, but spending quality time with them or at least watching them shop will help you to understand how and why they make purchase decisions. You'll also get a better handle on what they chose not to buy. This is a particularly good way to identify styling issues, in addition to fit and quality problems.

The most tragic failures occur when a designer creates a beautiful product that's poorly executed in terms of fit or quality. In fashion seeing, touching, and trying on products before buying is important to consumers. And while better online merchandising and product visualizations have undoubtedly enhanced the e-commerce experience in recent years, it's still very far from replicating the feeling of interacting with products in a physical store. Online, finding the right fit also remains a significant problem. So, if you are lucky enough to be selling product out of your own store, spend as much time as possible on the floor interacting with your customers. And if possible, when visiting your accounts, observe (or work!) the sales floor.

Posting a feedback link on your website or via social media is another quick and easy way to get more structured thoughts from your customers. You may be surprised how happy your customers will be to help you out.

Understanding the demographics is not as important as understanding the psychographics of the consumer, like the reason they buy things. If we take this last economic crisis, we see that designer-shoes (which are classified as shoes over $800), never lost a hiccup in sales. Never! This means that during the crisis, many people value system were different. They might have given up car services, lunch dates, and exotic vacations but, they weren't giving up their shoes. Also, understanding price resistance, where they spend money, and knowing their shopping routine is extremely important.

> *Price resistance is very scientific and people spend all day long studying why people will pay more for some thing and less for something else.*

> *Think of it this way when you wake up in the morning and you want to buy a cardigan. You go to the store, you try on a couple of them and you look at the price point and you say to yourself is this item too expensive or this is the right price, but you didn't wake up saying to yourself, I'm going to pay $12.95 for a cardigan sweater.*

Bridging the psychographics of the consumer with marketing is a great thing. Calvin Klein said during an interview, "There are some intelligent and sophisticated people working in the marketing sector, selling positive and important ideas back to us in the form of branding".

Ask yourself; what is the nefarious force that leads us to pay more for a garment that we know is no better in terms of quality than its no-brand substitute? Perhaps some alchemy of peer group opinion, magazine advertising and publicity makes it more attractive, even if no one will see the logo. The reality is if you engage with your customers at the retail level or via social media you will have more loyal customers. Better yet, customers who engage with your brand report spending 20% to 40% more on your brand. How can your business see this sort of boost? First off, you need to expand your concept of "customer service." It's no longer an isolated section of your business model but part of a larger customer engagement strategy. That's because responsibilities that traditionally fell to the marketing and product teams now fall into the realm of customer service. Now, your bottom line is riding on your ability to deliver excellent service while you are meaningfully engaging customers.

In order to build loyal relationships that extend and last, you need to understand the basic principles of the new definition of customer engagement and put them into action. Customer engagement is no longer a series of one-off experiences—it's an ongoing dialogue. You have to be a good listener in the digital age, and that requires a new set of skills. It means listening to customers who are already having conversations about brands – yours and others—in traditional online channels as well as over the social media. So jump into those conversations in a genuine and human way. Foster trust and form relationships through open, honest interactions over time, interactions that create positive experiences and outcomes for your customers. Positive outcomes include answering questions, solving problems, hearing ideas and supporting them (when possible), and also amplifying praise.

Although communication with your customers is an ongoing dialogue, you need not be chatting just for the sake of it. When you engage your customers, have a goal in mind, whether it's improving your product or nurturing loyalty and increasing sales. While traditionally the product team manages product and marketing is responsible for increasing brand awareness and driving sales, the lines are blurred now. Nurturing an ongoing and genuine relationship with your customers will naturally make a major impact in both these arenas.

Naturally, how you engage with your customers impacts how customers view your brand. Studies show, 70% of Americans are willing to spend an average of 13% more with companies who they feel provide above-par customer service. That means that all your customer engagement efforts should lead clearly in the direction of resolution. Know what the outcome should be, and provide your customers with clear tools that make it easy and efficient for them to get what they need. When you put control in their hands, you're more likely to be able to meet their needs, but you also win their trust, and ultimately, you build the loyal customer base you need to grow and succeed.

Notes:

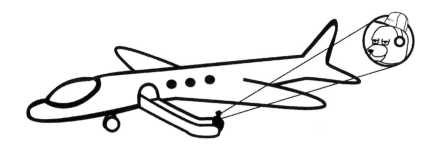

CHAPTER 6
NOT A DESK JOB

Fashion is not a desk job. Given that most small brands have limited industry awareness and contacts, building a wholesale business often involves hiring an experienced in-house sales-person or working with an external showroom. This person, or agency, will generally leverage their networks and relationships to make sure you get appointments with the right buyers, present your product effectively and ultimately secure orders. No matter what you decide, make sure you do your research and get lots of referrals. Don't be afraid to talk to existing clients.

Your wholesale representative, whether in-house or out-sourced, will ultimately be speaking for your brand, so make sure the fit is right. And even if you are not driving sales yourself, stay close to the wholesale process it is key to understanding how your collections are received and what can be done to improve them.

Avoid consignment at all cost. While most sales are not that — meaning the account actually buys the product from you — some accounts will only consign the merchandise. This means you still own the goods until they are sold, at which point you will split the revenues with your host. If the product doesn't sell, you carry the entire burden of the upfront costs. Beware consignment deals can put an emerging brand at great financial risk.

With a sales team in place, you will be able to take part in the various markets and sales-related events that occur on a regular basis around the world. While they can make a big short-term splash, fashion shows and presentations can be a big expense for emerging designers and are sometimes hard to justify, given the limited resulting sales uplift. Before you decide to invest in a show, consider the audience you are trying to reach and what you will reasonably gain in press, credibility and ultimately sales. Don't be afraid to seek out low cost or subsidized venues and other options. Endorsements and sponsorships can also be an effective way to offset these costs. And remember, not every designer needs to stage a fashion show. Wait until you have a clear message you want to send. Look-books and line sheets are a nice selling and marketing tool. But these can be extremely expensive to produce. So, think creatively, consider putting the file on a branded flash-drive or referring buyers to your website (or brand boom site).

It does not matter the route you choose, get out there and see the state of the world for yourself. While buyers and company executives will give you good intelligence, the sales associates who work on the front lines can also be valuable in painting a vivid picture of how your product performs on the shop floor.

As an added bonus, you may be pleasantly surprised by the attention your product gets on the floor once an associate is better acquainted with you. You should also spend some time observing your peers (also known as competitors). Most customers have a finite amount of money to spend on fashion and it's important to understand what other brands competing for that same share of wallet are doing and, in particular, which types of products seem to be performing the best. A good case study to look at regarding total customer interaction such as; Branding -Marketing - Sales - Integration - Fulfillment - Distribution, is Zara. See below how they have created a seamless, efficient, and successful fashion brand.

Zara Example

Synergy between business and operations strategy

Zara's overarching strategy is achieving growth through diversification with vertical integrations. It adapts couture designs, manufactures, distributes, and retails clothes within 2 weeks of the original design first appearing on catwalks. The company owns its supply chain and competes on its speed to market, literally embodying the idea of "fast fashion".

Just in time production

The retail giant delivers fashionable and trendy numbers catered for different tastes through a controlled and integrated process – just in time.

Zara keeps a significant amount of its production in-house and makes sure that its own factories reserve 85 percent of their capacity for in-season adjustments. In-house production allows the organization to be flexible in the amount, frequency, and variety of new products to be launched. The company often relies heavily on sophisticated fabric sourcing, cutting, and sewing facilities nearer to its design headquarters in Spain.

The wages of these European workers are higher than those of their developing-world counterparts, but the turnaround time is miraculous.

Zara also commits six months in advance to only 15 to 25 percent of a season's line. And it only locks in 50 to 60 percent of its line by the start of the season, meaning that up to 50 percent of its clothes are designed and manufactured smack in the middle of the season.

If a certain style or design suddenly become the rage, Zara reacts quickly, designs new styles, and gets them into stores while the trend is still peaking.

Store managers communicate customer feedback on what shoppers like, what they dislike, and what they're looking for. That data is instantly funneled back to Zara's designers who begin sketching on the spot.

Zara also has extra capacity on hand to respond to demand as it develops and changes. For example, it operates typically 4.5 days per week around the clock on full capacity, leaving some flexibility for extra shifts and temporary labor to be added when needed.

This then translates to frequent shipments and higher numbers of customer visits to the stores, creating an environment of shortage and opportunity.

This strategy allows Zara to sell more items at full price because of the sense of scarcity and exclusiveness the company exudes. Zara's total cost is minimized because merchandise that is marked down is reduced dramatically as compared to competitors.

Zara gets 85 percent of the full price on its clothes, while the industry average is 60 to70 percent. Unsold items account for less than 10 percent of its stock, compared with an industry average of 17 to 20 percent.

"Most companies are riddled with penny-wise, pound-foolish decisions to reduce cost," says Kasra Ferdows, a professor at Georgetown University's McDonough School of Business. "Zara understands that if they don't have to discount as much, they can spend money on other things. They can see the benefit of this certainty and rhythm in the supply chain."

This is also the reason why Zara can afford the extra labor and shipping costs needed to accommodate and satisfy changes in seasonality and customer demand.

Inventory management

Zara is fully aware of the saying, "inventory = death". It avoids piling up inventory in any part of its supply chain from raw materials to finished products.

Inventory optimization models are put in place to help the company to determine the quantity that should be delivered to every single one of its retail stores via shipments that go out twice every week. The stock delivered is strictly limited, ensuring that each store only receives just want they need. This goes towards the brand image of being exclusive while avoiding the build-up of unpopular stock.

This quick in-season turnaround, from production facilities located close to Zara's distribution headquarters in Spain, allows Zara to ship more often and in smaller batches. If the design Zara hastily creates in an attempt to chase the latest trend does not in fact sell well, little harm is done.

The batch is small, so there's not a ton of unsold inventory to get rid of. And because the failed experiment is over in a jiffy, there's still time to try a different style, and then a different one after that.

Centralized logistics

"The secret to their success has been centralization," says Felipe Caro, an associate professor at the University of California at Los Angeles's Anderson School of Management and a business adviser to the company. "They can make decisions in a very coordinated manner."

Zara sticks to a deep, predictable and fast rhythm, based around order fulfillment to stores.

Each Zara outlet sends in two orders per week on specific days and timing. Trucks leave at specific times and shipments arrive in stores at specific times. Garments are already labeled and priced upon destination.

As a result of this clearly defined rhythm, every staff involved (from design to procurement, production, distribution, and retail) knows the timeline and how their activities pan out with respect to other functions. That certainly also extends to Zara customers, who know when to visit stores for fresh new garments.

Solid distribution network

Zara's strong distribution network enables the company to deliver goods to its European stores within 24 hours, and to its American and Asian outlets in less than 40 hours.

According to Nelson Fraiman, a Columbia Business School professor who wrote a 2010 case study about Zara, the retail giant can get a product out from concept to store in just 15 days, while the industry standard is 6 months. At Zara, change doesn't disrupt the system; it's part of the system.

This brand's success story shows the strength of its operations. Its cross-functional operations strategy, coupled with its vertically integrated supply chain, enables mass production under push control, leading to well-managed inventories, lower markdowns, higher profitability, and value creation for shareholders in the short and long term.

Courtesy of www.tradegecko.com

Sales are the core of any fashion business. You can have great product and excellent visibility, but without underlying sales your business can never work. As painful and painstaking as it can be, a successful sales strategy requires your close attention, so don't leave it entirely to someone else.

Notes:

CHATER 7
PRODUCTION

For most small fashion brands and start-ups, finding sources for production is the most challenging element to get right. Too often, early-stage businesses put it off until it's too late, and sometimes find themselves with orders to fulfill, but nobody to produce them. This is something to avoid at all cost. Once you have taken orders, you must be able to fulfill them, or you risk scaring away retailers for years to come. Remember, this is a small industry and everybody talks.

While there are endless options for production, both domestic and international, finding quality suppliers can be difficult, especially in the UK and USA, where many top young fashion designers are based. As a result, many in the industry tend to be secretive and protective of their production sources. In recent years, producers in France and Italy have become more open to working with young designers. But your orders (in small, unpredictable quantities) may tend to get pushed to the back of the order queue, meaning that your deliveries may be later than bigger brands, which can negatively impact sell-through rates and vendor relationships.

With so much competition for vendors, it's essential to make sure you can secure production before you invest time and money in the design process, sales process and marketing costs. How can you track down production resources? As with most things in fashion, it comes down to leveraging your relationships and seeking out help wherever you can find it:

Former Partners: If you've worked for another company previously, especially a larger one, some of your former producers may be willing to work with you, or at least make a referral.

Accounts: Often a retailer will have preferred production partners that their other accounts work with. They may even use them for their own private label product, and, if you ask nicely, they may be willing to make some introductions.

Sample Makers: Many small manufacturing labs or factories that create samples often have associated production facilities, or know the best local manufacturers. Use them as a resource as they may be able to point you in the right direction.

Fashion Schools: If you are a student or alumnus of a fashion school, check in with your professors and tutors to see what resources are available to you. They may also have relationships you can leverage.

Friends and Colleagues: It never hurts to ask. But beware you may not get a straight answer.

Online Resources: There are some very helpful sites that, for a fee, will give ratings and testimonials on apparel and textile manufacturers. Panjiva.com is a great example, although you may be hard-pressed to find top-quality resources if you operate at the luxury end of the business.

Another good reason to identify your production partner early in the process is because their execution capabilities and associated costs need to be figured into your early design decisions, and ultimately into your pricing.

If you've followed my advice from earlier in this book, you should have already set wholesale and retail pricing targets for your product. Then by simple comparisons of these prices to your quoted costs, you should be able to tell whether they will allow you to make enough profit-margin on each item, at the right level of quality. Many designers ask what a reasonable margin target should be. The answer, of course, varies depending on the size of your business, its overhead, development, sampling costs and many other factors.

Most companies try to achieve close to 50 percent margins at wholesale and over 70 percent in retail. But again, there are no hard and fast rules, as each circumstance requires different treatment. Remember that not all factories will have all the raw materials, fabrics and trims required to construct your product. If procurement falls on your company, you will need to source these yourself, and in doing so, incur costs that will likely need to be paid on an accelerated timeline.

Suppliers will require some sort of deposit or prepayment to cover raw materials and/or the labor needed for production. Whatever balance remains will usually be required once the goods are ready to ship.

Some suppliers will be flexible on terms, allowing you to delay these payments for weeks to months which will help your cash flow, as you are not likely to get paid by your accounts or customers for some time. Always ask for terms so you can give yourself some cushion on payments. And remember, whatever arrangements you agree on with your suppliers should always be captured in an official Purchase Order that should detail all transaction and delivery terms.

In order to get started with production, you will need to create or designate an approved sample to work by. This "sew by" sample, technical design, or design prototype, is the model by which the factory will use to create "bulk" production. If you are an apparel company, you will use these samples to define construction guidelines, as well as fit specifications and the grading of sizes up and down. When production is in process, it's important to monitor quality, as compared to your samples, which are what buyers will use to write their orders. The single best way to do this is to visit the facility regularly. This is obviously made easier when producing locally, but do not underestimate the value of an investment in travel to see production before shipping. Depending on the situation, you may be able to conduct fittings on test or bulk units to make sure that they are executing correctly. If this is possible, it is highly advisable. If you are unable to visit your facilities, there are third party auditors that can oversee quality control for a fee. When goods are ready and approved to be released, you will likely have them shipped or delivered. Some companies will "drop ship" directly to their own retail stores or accounts. Most often, the goods are received in an office or distribution warehouse.

Once you take possession of the final products, you should make sure to pull some (or all) of the units to check for quality on execution. This extra time and money is well spent considering that your customer or account is likely to return any faulty or ill-fitting product. Remember to have a clear understanding of any packing parameters required by specific accounts, as failure to adhere to these parameters can result in charge backs and even order cancellations. All in all, production can be the most complicated and cumbersome part of running a fashion business. If you have the resources to hire an experienced production manager, they will often be able to bring both know-how and sourcing contacts to your company. In fact, a production specialist is often one of the first hires a growing brand will make. Production is consistently one of the most in-demand skills in the fashion industry if you have a mind for managing complex processes and logistics, and an eye for product.

Notes:

CHAPTER 8
OFF THE BEATEN PATH

Opening a boutique can be a great investment, as the general public is always on the lookout for new fashions and great deals on existing designer clothes. But there's more to running a successful boutique than having a sharp sense of style and a passion for fashion. You need to select a location, maintain your supply lines, price your clothing to make a profit, buy your fashions, merchandising your store, and create a selling culture - as well as manage every other aspect of your business efficiently to maximize your profits.

LOCATION
One reason boutiques go out of business is because of location, not because of a few bad collections, bad weather, or a bad employee. It's the location.

You must wait until you find the right location; the money you think you're saving on rent by being off the beaten path, you will make up in advertising, promotions, and discounts. Look for a shopping district - it is very different from a tourist district.

For example: Times Square, New York City. Times Square, has approximately 300,000 people cross that corner every single week. Morgan Stanley is there, the W hotel is $600 a night, but it's not shopping traffic. If you look at just the shopping bags on the street, you will notice most of the shopping bags in Times Square are I Love New York t-shirts, two for $10, and the M&M store. The area is all about the tourist experience.

Also, be careful with your real estate agents because they're not usually your friend, and I mean that in the most honest way. They're doing a job and that's to sell you property. They may advise you that you want to be next to the supermarket, the post office, the bank, a popular restaurant, and yes while all of those places have inherited traffic, it's not shopping traffic.

Think about the last time you went to the supermarket, the post office, the gym, or even your favorite restaurant. Do you think the average shopper goes to one of these places and then says, "Okay, I'm going to go clothes shopping"? Probably not. And you don't want to be that store that everybody sees but nobody has the time to visit. Lesson: a good location is not necessarily a visible location.

See how you would fit into the local economy. See how you will complement other stores and always look for a national chain. Whenever I walk into a Gap, a Banana Republic or one of the nationals, I can get some of the employees to give me heads-up on when the best time for foot traffic is, how the business is performing, and more inside information. Remember you want to be in a business that makes money

Supply Chain

Now you have to ask yourself, "What am I going to sell?" In the beginning, a lot of new store owners will have a concept, but do not know what kind of products to sell. For now, I want you to ask yourself a few questions. The first thing is what's the need in my area? It's nice to find what complements the area.

> *I'll give you a perfect example why: if nothing exists like that in your area, there's a reason why. A couple of years ago a store owner came to me and said she had a very cute doggy boutique, at the height of the miniature doggy craze when Paris Hilton was carrying around Tinkerbell. She had a really cute set-up and she had a really cute groomer but sales were non-existent. The minute that she told me her location, I understood why. She was next to a 10-block building complex in New York City that doesn't allow pets. That's why there were no pet stores in her area.*

Sometimes it's obvious, sometimes it's not so obvious. You have to supply the need of the community. Also keep in mind some fashion brands might have exclusives already in the area, meaning they already sell a couple of retailers and they don't want to over-saturate the brand so they might not be willing to sell to you. The bottom line is you have to figure out if it's a product that's unique enough in your area, if you can make money selling it, and if you can actually supply it. At the end of the day, every inch of your store needs to make money for you, so understanding the sales per square foot is very important.

Your open-to-buy, which is your actual budget, is just as important. Your open-to-buy is like your checkbook, where every month you write a check to yourself regarding how much merchandise you can buy and need to buy for your store. Of course, the last one is return on investment. Everything that you put in your store, everything that you buy for your store, everything that you do that's related to your store, has to have a return on investment.

Pricing your wares

Nobody likes to talk about math but, math is probably the second most important thing in running a store. You need to know your math!

There are hundreds of formulas, but some of the formulas that you need to know are:

✓Retail Mark-up (Markup ($) = Retail Price – Cost),

✓Sales-to-Stock Ratio (Sales-to-Stock = Beginning of Month Stock ÷ Sales for the Month),

✓Sales-per-Square Foot (this is incredibly important because so many stores spend a lot of usage of retail space by putting sofas and chairs and play corners for little kids).

For Example: I want to tell you a quick story about one of my clients that I had a few years ago. Her husband called the office. She had four other businesses prior to them coming to me. She had been a stylist, an antiques dealer, a personal home decorator, and owned a gallery. Her husband said, "Well, now in this venture, we have to make money. We have to make money because I can't afford to keep throwing money into these other businesses." This time she wanted to open up a lingerie store. The lingerie business is really great because your two competitors are Victoria's Secret and Macy's, so it's easy to compete in this niche. She sits down and tells me the location of her store is in a very conservative town in Virginia. The first thing that she said is that she wants to carry La Perla. La Perla is the most expensive racy underwear that you could possibly purchase on the planet. I said, "Well, why do you want to carry that brand?" She said "Because my friends and I wear it." We chatted a little bit, and I said, "La Perla may not be the best pick for you." I gave her some suggestions, something like shape-wear-- you should have seen the look of horror on her face, "like shape-wear -- who wears that?" Then I said, "Listen, because it's a smaller town, maybe you need some sleepwear." She said, "What, you mean like teddies?" I said, "No, like pajama tops and sweatshirts." She said no (she was breaking the number one rule, which is not buying things for yourself -- you should be buying the things that sell.) Fast forward, we buy La Perla and I figure after three months, we'll look at the numbers.

The numbers won't lie to us. Three months went by. I came back to the store and we look specifically at that vendor, La Perla. Fifty percent of it was sold at 50 percent off. Twenty percent of it was missing from the store. Somebody mentioned she took it home, which translates to she stole from the store. Thirty percent was sold at 20 percent, that's the discount that she was giving her friends.

When we looked at the math, La Perla was not making any money whatsoever for her and her store. Then she says to me, "But, everybody calls up and asks for the brand." I said, "What do you mean they call up? Are you advertising? ;She said, No." Because it's a big national / international brand that advertises in popular magazines, they would list the brand "Available in these fine stores" and one of her fine stores was listed. People would call up and say, "Hey, do you have the tulip bra?" "Yes, we do we have the tulip bra, come on in." They would come in, see that the tulip bra is $400 and say, "What else do you have?" In the industry, this is called a loss leader. She didn't intend for La Perla to be a loss leader but that is exactly what it became. A loss leader is when we know from the beginning we're not making money on an item, but we bring it in because it attracts people to buy our other brands and our private label brand which are very important because the margins are better. In the end she adjusted her product mix but continued to carry La Perla to create traffic.

Buyer

Let's talk about how to be a buyer; there is a big difference between being a buyer and having somebody sell to you. You don't want anybody selling to you, you want to be able to put your grown up pants on and be the buyer. You want to have the final choice in everything that you choose for your store. When you are at a tradeshow, the first thing is to take a look around at all the products. It's important to walk every aisle row by row even if it's a product category that you are not used to carrying in your store. Ask the vendors if it's okay to thumb through their merchandise. You want to able to look and choose, you want to able to look at merchandise and pick a retail price that you think your customer will pay.

Next you want to ask "can you give me a range of price points?" Some of the vendors are going to say "sure our t-shirts start at a dollar and go to a hundred dollars." They are not giving you a price range. There are many amateurs that waste the vendors' time and these tradeshows are very expensive, so really be professional and know what you are doing and know the right questions. You want to be more assertive and you want to be firm so you might say, "let's try this again - give me an idea of your blended t-shirt prices and your casual t-shirts prices" and they'll likely give you a better idea of their price point.

The next question is "what is your cancel date" and this is important because you want to be able to control when the merchandise comes into your store. If you are buying goods for Easter you want to make sure they are in the store six weeks before. You want a cancel date that is at least six weeks before that day. A cancel date; in legal terminology means the last possible date that the vendor is allowed to ship to you without you canceling the order. You also need a start date. You have to stay in control of your order, so it's really important that you put a start date and a cancel date. For example, let's say we are placing an order for Valentine's Day (February14th). We want the goods six weeks before, so we want a start date of December 30th with a cancel date of January 10th. That means that you still have enough time to get the goods into store, tag them, price them and put them out and be able to sell. A start date and a cancel date are very important to have on your order.

The next question you want to ask about is Freight On Board FOB. You want to know if you are responsible for paying for this shipment. Usually the FOB will be somewhere in the United States--if it's coming from Canada, South America, or France you want to be aware that you may incur additional charges of TCP and Duties.

Once you determine the shipping you want to discuss the terms. Basically when you are a small company and first starting out it's going to be on credit card terms. My advice to you is to never give a credit card at a tradeshow and make sure that you have an invoice that you can match up with your order. You should write your own orders on your own order forms, the reason for this is so that you have uniformity while playing by your own rules. You can then send your credit card authorization form along with your invoice. Your credit card authorization form should say "you will never charge my credit card again without my written authorization and you will ship my goods within three days of the credit card being charged." This is really important; you really want to emphasize this. Buy what you're comfortable buying. Let's say that the minimum order is five hundred dollars and you look at it quickly and you can see you're only up to three hundred dollars. It's okay to tell the vendor, "Listen, I'm new, you're new to me; let's build a working relationship together. I'm comfortable buying three hundred dollars worth of merchandise, can you work with me?" I promise you ninety-nine percent of the time they are going to say it's okay and they are going to work with you. There's always that one guy that is going to say no; my advice is take your orders home and then fax them in later. The idea is that when you are buying you are the buyer; don't let people sell you. Remember, you are the backbone of this industry, you are the risk taker, you are the one who is going to try a new or emerging designer. You are the one who is going to go out of your way to be the best advocate for the unknown. Which leads me to another valuable component, merchandising!

Merchandising

Merchandising a retail store has a tremendous amount of science and psychology behind it.

They tell us that we should merchandise for the five senses (hearing, touch, taste, smell, and sight), but the truth is, we have more than five senses. We have our sense of well-being. You know that feeling that you get when something's not right? We have our sense of balance. Have you ever walked into a store and felt dizzy because there was so much clutter everywhere? We have our sense of temperature, of being too hot or too cold. All of those subconscious senses are very important when we're merchandising the store. One of the things that I like to talk about is how we set the environment and how we set the mood in the store; music, lighting, smell are important. I would like to use Hollister as an example.

For Example: A few years ago, the Hollister retail team decided that they wanted to study what are the negative factors in the shopping experience of kids from 9 to18 years old. If you think about it, kids 9 to18, what could possibly be the negative factor? When they did this study, they followed a child from the parking lot to inside the store and they realized that the negative factor was the parent. How do we get rid of the parent? Obviously, if the kid is 9 years old he can't drive himself to the mall, so he might be able to get dropped off at the mall, but most likely he's with a parent. So they focused on the retail environment; they made the store dark, like a cave, and made the music so loud and unbearable that anybody over the age of 20 cannot spend more than two minutes in the store (it is documented).). So as a parent, what do you do? You walk into the store and say, "Oh my God, I can't take the music. It's too dark in here. I'll wait for you outside." Every single Hollister is positioned outside of what we call short-term parking. The short-term parking could be a bench, a very simple bench in a very low-brow mall, or it could be a recliner with a guy playing the piano in the center of the mall. They purposely placed the stores in these locations so the parent could come and sit.

Typically, a parent gives the child 10 minutes to shop; in that 10 minutes the child can usually run around the store and increase the sales or units per transaction (UPT), by one item, so that means that they've doubled sales by changing the retail environment. That was very successful, so they came up with a strategy to the increase this 10-minute clock. In phase two they made sure that every new Hollister is two doors down from a Starbucks, because now the parent comes out of the store. They look around. There's a Starbucks. "Let's walk over to the Starbucks." All of this is a very scientific process and based on increasing time in the retail location. They realized that it takes seven minutes from the front of the store to get your Starbucks, and come back, so now they've added seven minutes to the 10-minute clock and they have increased sales by one more item. They've increased the sales two items from the original one item by placement, sound, and sight. This is how important it is when you are merchandising your stores.

It is important when a person walks into the store that they don't feel like they're trapped; make sure you have a focus wall; it is usually the back wall. Your store layout is important because it sets the tone for the entire shopping experience. Let's take a look at Target. When you walk into Target, there's a big row of registers. If you listen really carefully, you can even hear the casino ka-chink sounds. People are lined up, so already subconsciously you're telling yourself, "Wow, everybody's lined up, everybody's shopping, I better get to business." Target reinforces it one more way. The minute you walk in, over to the right there's always those dollar bins. Even though you've told yourself all the way from the parking lot, "We're not going to go near the dollar bins," there's like a magnet on your shopping cart that takes you right to it, so now you start picking things up. Oh my God, it's so cute. It's only a dollar. It's so cute, it's only a dollar.

It's okay, it's only a dollar, so subconsciously, you have just programmed yourself into thinking that everything in the store is cheap and cute and you'd better get shopping.

A curated environment is critically important in up-selling the customer. Let's go to Gucci, let's go to Louis Vuitton. Where's the register? It's hidden in the back. Sometimes it's completely off the floor, because when you look at that register, you're not thinking cheap and cute, you're thinking, I'm spending a lot of money. Think about the last time you went into a high fashion store that you were not familiar with, and you said to yourself, "Oh my God, this store is so expensive," without looking at a single price point. It was the retail environment that gave you that impression. Psychology placements, like the mannequins, who we call the silent salesperson, is very important. When merchandising your store, always keep in mind the psychology behind it.

Sales

So now you have your store. You have the perfect location. You have great product. You have a great staff, but you still need to train them in sales, not rely on a commission sales model. I'll tell you why. We've all had an experience when we've helped ourselves at a store that pays employees based on commission, and then at the last minute somebody comes over and says, "Hey, my name is Margie." And you think, "Well, Margie, where were you five minutes ago when I needed a size?" Solely relying on a commission-based sales model means that you are relying on employees that may be really ambitious or really lazy, which can affect your sales and customer satisfaction.

I am a fan of building a team and I really feel that when you have a team together it becomes like the show "Survivor".

If one man isn't pulling his own weight, they vote him off the island and that's really what you want. In order to get there you have to recruit correctly and you have to spend the time to train them

A quick sales training tip involves how you greet the customer. In New York City, a head nod is a big greeting. That's enough. The other thing about New York City is that I could be 2 feet in front of you and I'm not in your face because 2 minutes ago I was shoulder-to-shoulder with somebody on a subway. But in the South or in other parts of the country, you need to have a distance because they live in big houses, they drive in cars by themselves and they're used to having a lot of space. Not being in their face is really important when you greet. The tone of your voice is important.

Again, going back to New York, a quick, "Hey," is enough. It's a greeting. But, in the South, a really warm, embracing greeting like, "Hey, how are you? You're not from around here are you? Let me tell you about my store." As a Southerner, that would probably be appropriate. Understanding who you're talking to culturally has to be done in seconds. I know there's a lot of political correctness about profiling. So you have to be very good at your job, and you have to be able to approach people in a culturally competent manner.

I'm sure you've heard a lot about Omni-channel retailing, and it might sound a little scary, but in a nutshell it's being everywhere that your customer is. If they're standing at line at the movies or they're at the restaurant or they're home in bed, they want to be able to shop from their iPhones, SmartPhones, Facebook, or the internet. The interesting thing about it is that a lot of retailers think that it cannibalizes their brick-and-mortar business but it doesn't. It actually enhances it.

Having the consumer experience at retail is very different from online shopping but one really enhances the other. It's not an option in today's retail business to be without this Omni-channel presence. There probably hasn't been a better time in the last couple of decades to open up your retail shop. With the technology of Omni-channel retailing where you can reach your customers 24 hours a day, 7 days a week in all parts of the world with the availability of a wonderful retail space. They actually look like small lifestyle centers. Today's consumer is hungry for something new that's well crafted, interesting, has the wow power, and the customer service that only an independent retailer can provide. There hasn't been a better time to open up your own store.

Notes:

CHAPTER 9
SELECTING AN E-COMMERCE PLATFORM

While it's clear to most emerging fashion brands that there
is a compelling opportunity in e-commerce, their quandary
is usually how and when to launch. This is often exacerbated
by the level of investment required to get started and a lack
of technical expertise. Luckily, there are some great new tools
available that enable easy setup of an e-commerce site at highly
affordable rates. Platforms like Shopify, SquareSpace, and Tictail
offer off-the-shelf, plug-and-play options for companies new to
e-commerce. These services require few technical skills to set
up and are extremely simple to use, though they are templates,
with little scope for customization. As for cost, however, most
offer simple revenue sharing schemes or low monthly fees.
Open source e-commerce platform Magneto is another, more
flexible, option, though deployment requires greater technical
expertise.

Generally speaking, these kinds of platforms are ideal for brands with expected sales below $1 million annually. If your business is expected to sell over $1 million online, annually, you may want to consider more advanced platforms, such as Demand Ware, Venda, or Sellect. These services are more flexible and offer more robust, customizable feature sets, including easy-to-manage, drag-and-drop merchandising tools, but require significant investment to deploy. Before choosing an e-commerce platform, you should be clear about your specific business goals and sales targets.

An equally important point to consider before you build a website is who is going to run it on a day-to-day basis. As with any storefront, e-commerce sites require constant management, as new product arrives and marketing messages evolve. If you or your team will be managing your e-commerce business day-to-day, the site must allow for easy, regular changes. Make sure you fully understand the content management system that accompanies the platform you choose, so you can operate the site and train others.

> *Every e-commerce platform should also come with a Customer Relationship Management (CRM) system, which will help you to collect and organize customer data. It's very important to carefully vet these systems, as the direct relationship you develop with your customers through an e-commerce site can be one of the strongest tools in growing your business and result in significant sales lift.*

No matter which platform you choose, you will need to design a compelling website. With simpler platforms, which allow for little customizing, you might consider doing this yourself. But more likely, site design will be undertaken by a professional web designer on your team, or by an outsourced individual or agency.

While I could write an entire book on the finer points of building a great online store, I recommend that you work closely with vetted professionals to create a site that is not only a proper reflection of your brand, but also offers an engaging and enjoyable user experience. Working with a trained user experience professional, or UX, is as important as working with a visual designer. Be wary of agencies that tell you this function is not needed. Your site should also work easily and gracefully across multiple types of devices, like smartphones and tablets. In 2013, around 15 percent of total e-commerce sales in the US were made from "post-PC" devices, with 65 percent of those coming from tablets, according to Emarketer. By 2017, sales from mobile and tablet devices are expected to account for 25 percent of total purchases. With this in mind, it's crucial that your e-commerce presence be optimized for these platforms. But rather than designing a separate mobile sites or apps, I suggest building your site using "responsive design," an approach that enables your site to automatically detect your user's device and adjust the experience to different display sizes and forms of interaction (like touch screens). Remember, your e-commerce site is nothing without content. Beautiful brand images and product photography are a must. I recommend that you work with a trained photographer to shoot these images and remember to capture multiple angles. Zoom and 360 degree views of the product are also nice to have.

Inventory management is a critical part of operating an e-commerce site. For many brands, this site is their first foray into the direct-to-consumer sales channel. While this has several benefits, as outlined above, investing in inventory without the guarantee of confirmed orders can be a risky, cash-intensive undertaking.

Many young brands simply allocate a predetermined percentage of their offering to the online channel. While this approach may work for the inaugural season, I recommend a more precise planning process whereby you use past sales data for similar styles, look at traffic growth from season to season, and consider the overall "visibility" of each particular product.

As can be expected, an item featured on the homepage, or one that might be planned for heavy press exposure, is likely to sell at a higher volume. One of the benefits of an e-commerce site is the ability to manage your own liquidation channel. Whether it's unsold units, excess inventory from returns, or even extra samples, you can utilize your new store to move goods. But it's important that you do this in a way that does not damage full price sales, so be conscious of over emphasizing sales.

An e-commerce site must also be coupled to a fulfillment platform that can process orders, ship to customers and accept any returns. When some small brands first launch their sites, they fulfill goods right from their offices, or apartments! Other brands partner with a third-party logistics center that will hold the goods, manage shipping and process returns. Often times, these warehouses do not manage customer service, so it falls on the brand to answer phone calls and emails from their customers. While this might seem a headache, it can often help a brand uncover important feedback that should be incorporated into future product designs and company strategies.

Finally, an e-commerce site cannot survive without ongoing promotion and traffic generation. There are many methods to achieve this. Some specific methods to consider relating to e-commerce are search engine optimization (SEO), search engine marketing (SEM), affiliate marketing, email, and ongoing promotion via social media. According to a study of Forrester, released in 2006, more than 93% of traffic on a brand's website comes from the search engines. Thus, the main goal for apparel brands has to be to improve their visibility on Google or other search engines such as Yahoo, Bing, Baidu in China or Yandex in Russia. Basically, there has to be a distinction between "natural" or "earned" results. Several rules have to be understood to improve the "natural" ranking of the brands' website. Nevertheless, "organic" results are not enough anymore. Fashion and luxury brands have to invest into online advertising services (SEM) such as Google AdWords, so as to be competitive.

Luxury brands try to stand out and use a lot of flash or animated content. Such websites, however, are destructive for Search Engine Optimization. Every fashion brand manager should have a look at their blank HTML code to identify if there is enough data to read for a web-crawler or spider.

Example: A case which could be improved, is that of Tom Ford (Score: 58.77). There are many pictures on their website and the HTML code is less than average. Hence the web-crawlers have less information to read and analyze, because there is not much text on the website. Thus, the crawler ranks the website as less important since there is not a lot of information (text content) available for crawling. (credit: fashionbi.com)

Example II: Analyzing the website of Prada (Score: 49.11) the keyword density is highly related to language keywords such as "English", "francais", "deutsch", which, in the long-run is highly fruitful for the brand to get visibility on not only a global search engine but also the local ones (such as google.fr, google.de etc.). Hence, it is definitely mandatory to have your website translated in more than one language, besides, of course, English. (credit: fashionbi.com)

Another way to improve fashion brand's SEO is to gather relevant backlinks. For instance, if a fashion bloggers put a link on their blog to the fashion brands official website, this tells Google that this particular brand is relevant. A few years ago, there was a battle of spreading lots and lots backlinks. Nowadays, it is more controlled and hence, it is important to have few but worthwhile backlinks, on quality third-party websites. Having a backlink from a fashion blogger or other fashion related website with more traffic is much more worth for Google than having dozens of links on irrelevant websites. These days, Google is even punishing link buying, cloaking or other fraudulent intends - by completely cancelling the ranking for a page that tries to go into this direction, just to achieve SEO. According to marketing research about Bloggers Influence in Fashion & Luxury industry, a lot of brands try new ways to collaborate with fashion bloggers. Since product placement is already common these days, brands use Bloggers as Models, as Illustrators, as Co-editors or even their brand Ambassadors. All this can lead to good backlinks to support one's SEO.

> *Linkbaits is another way of spreading one's website across the internet and to obtain a higher significance for Google (or other search engines). Wikipedia is another resource of how to improve the fashion brands relevance for search engines. The info on a fashion brand has to appear on the entire first page of Google, when a viewer is searching any information related to that brand.*

Search engines are the biggest single source of visitors for almost every website. If you want your online platform to achieve any kind of success and bring increased sales and profitability, you need to get on the top of the search engines that are most used by your target audience.

Notes:

THE END

HELPFUL FASHION TERMS

A-line gown - Form fitting bodices that flare out from the waist-line to a full skirt. These gowns have a seamless waist.

A-line skirt/fit and flare skirt - A skirt that is fitted at the waist and flares out in an A-line or tulip shape at the hem.

Back drape - A length of material attached either at the shoulder or the waist that flows over the back to floor length. In some cases it is removable.

Back yoke - A fitted or shaped piece at the top of a skirt or at the shoulder of various garments.

Ball gown - Characterized by a very full skirt that begins at the waist and continues to a formal length. The skirt waist is seamed and can be of various styles.

Ballerina neckline - This is a low neckline that usually occurs with strapless or spaghetti strapped dresses.

Bandeau/tube top - A band-shaped covering for the breasts.
Basque waist/V-waist - This dropped waist starts at or just below the natural waistline, and dips in the center creating a "V" shape.

Bateau neck/boat neck - A high, wide, straight neckline that runs straight across the front and back, meeting at the shoulders; the same depth in the front and back.

Besom pockets - A pocket sewn inside the garment with access through a welted slit-type opening.

Bias cut - Cut diagonally across the grain of a fabric. Used to create garments that follow the body curves closely.

Bike tards - A close-fitting, one-piece garment from the top of the torso to the hem of the shorts.

Blazer - A long-sleeved sports jacket with lapels.

Bolero jacket - A loose, waist-length jacket open at the front.

Boot-cut - Cut below the belly button and slightly flares from the knee to the ankle.

Box-pleated - Two folds of fabric brought together to form a pleat.

Boy-leg - Shorts, undergarments, or swimwear that has a close fitting leg that reaches half way down the thigh.

Broomstick - A skirt or dress that is characterized by numerous pleats and crinkled material.

Camp pockets - Pockets that are sewn to the outside of the garment, usually squared off and characterized by seaming.

Cap sleeve - A small, short sleeve which sits on the shoulder, either forming a stiff cap or falling on to the arm to provide minimal coverage.

Capri pants - Fairly straight-cut pants, tapered to the mid-calf.
Cardigan jacket - A usually collarless sweater or jacket that opens the full length of the center front.

Cargo - Characterized by sporting a large pocket usually with a flap and a pleat.

Carpenter pants/shorts - Five-pocket pants characterized by a "hammer holder," a stretch of material connecting the outside seam to the back pocket.

Cathedral train - (Also known as a monarch train); a cascading train extending six to eight feet behind the gown, for the most formal weddings.

Chapel train - The most popular of all train lengths, it flows from three to four feet behind the gown.

Chemise/skimmer - A straight unbelted dress with varying sleeves and length.

Column skirt/straight skirt - Also referred to as a pencil skirt, this skirt is a straight line with no flare or fullness at the hem or waistline.

Concealed snap/velcro/button placket - A slit in a garment where closures are hidden.

Convertible collar - A rolled collar that can be worn open or closed. Sewn directly to the neckline.

Corset top/boned bodice - A form-fitting, usually strapless bodice with boning and either laces or snap closures, styled in the fashion of the ladies undergarment of the same name.

Cowl neck - A neckline featuring a piece of material attached to a garment at the neck, which may be used as a hood or draped loosely in a swag from shoulder to shoulder at the front neckline or back.

Crew neck - A round neck with ribbed banding that fits close to the base of the neck.

Crinoline - Petticoats stiffened with horse-hair to enable the bell-like skirts of the early nineteenth century that was eventually replaced with the bustle.

Cropped top/jacket - Hem is cut just above the waist.
Diamond neck - A diamond-shaped cutout that fastens at the front or back neckline.

Double-breasted - Having one-half of the front lapped over the other, and usually has a double row of buttons and a single row of buttonholes.

Double-tee top - A layered look with one T-shirt over another T-shirt.

Draped bodice - A extra piece of material is draped over the bustline.

Dropped waist/low waist - A waistline that is sewn below the body's natural waistline.

Dropped shoulders - Characterized by the shoulder/sleeve seam falling off the shoulder.

Empire seams - A seam that is sewn directly below the bustline.

Fishtail train - Fitted around the hips and flares out from the knee to the hemline.

Fitted point sleeve - A long, narrow sleeve that tapers to a point which rests against the back of the hand.

Flat-front pants - Straight pants, often seamless and pocket-less.
Form-fitting/slim-fit - Straight from waist to ankle except for a slight curve around the hip.

Gauntlets -Dress gloves extending above the wrist.
Gaucho - Wide-legged pants or divided skirt reaching mid-calf and worn with boots.

Halter top - A sleeveless bodice with a high choke or wrap neck that may be backless.

Handkerchief style - The hem of a blouse or skirt that is gently jagged to form flowing points.

Hip pockets - Pockets which are sewn on the front of the garment at hip height.

Hollywood waistband - Characterized by a full elasticized back and a side zipper/button closure.

Hook & Eye closure - A 2-part fastening device (as on a garment or a door) consisting of a metal hook that catches over a bar or into a loop.

Illusion bodice - A bodice made of sheer material giving the illusion of no bodice.

Illusion sleeve - A sleeve made of sheer material giving the illusion of no sleeve.

Intermission length/Hi-Lo - An intermission-length gown features a hem falling between the knees and ankle; the Hi-Lo variation is a gown of intermission length on the front and floor length or longer in the back.

Jewel neck - A high round neckline resting simply at the base of the neck.

Kangaroo pocket - A pocket formed by sewing a piece of cloth over the garment leaving two open ends.

Keyhole neck - A tear shaped or round cutout that fastens at the front or back neckline.

Kimono - A long robe with wide sleeves traditionally worn with a broad sash.

Leg-of-mutton sleeve - (Also known as a gigot sleeve) a loose, full sleeve, rounded from the shoulder to just below the elbow, then shaped to the arm, often ending in a point at the wrist.

Maillot - A woman's one-piece bathing suit.
Mandarin collar - A short, stand-up collar, adopted from the close-fitting Asian collar.

Mermaid - This skirt hugs the body until it reaches the knees or just below and then ends in a dramatic flare.

Natural waist - A seam or waistband that secures or falls at the natural curve of the body, which is the indentation between the hips and the ribcage.

Notched collar - A two-piece collar that can be only worn open.

Off-the-shoulder neck - A neckline that lies gently hovering across the top of the bustline with the shoulders uncovered or able to be seen through the sheer yoke of net or organza attached to a high collar.

Overskirt - A skirt worn over another skirt.

Peasant top - Romantic style often characterized with a low neckline, ruffles, or free flowing material.

Peek-a-boo - Any part of the garment which has been cut out to reveal skin.

Petticoat - An underskirt usually a little shorter than outer clothing and often made with a ruffled, pleated, or lace edge.

Pieced - A look created by sewing several pieces of material together to form the garment, much like a quilt.

Pinafore - Originally used to protect dresses from dirt, it was adopted as a fashion piece and worn as a sleeveless dress or over a blouse.

Princess seams - Seams that can be found in the front or the back of a garment that create a form-fitting shape.
Puckered bodice - Usually associated with tube tops, it provides a scrunchy look.

Princess seams - Seams that can be found in the front or the back of a garment that create a form-fitting shape.

Puckered bodice - Usually associated with tube tops, it provides a scrunchy look.

Puff sleeve/pouf sleeve - A full sleeve of varying lengths, created by generous gathering around the armhole.

Push-up jeans - Spandex in the jeans helps to lift and shape your rear.

Romper - A one-piece garment with the lower part shaped like bloomers.

Sarong skirt - Long cloth which is wrapped around the entire body.

Scoop neck/round neck - A low, U-shaped or round neckline.

Shawl collar - A one-piece collar which is turned down to form a continuous line around the back of the neck to the front.

Sheaths - Usually have straight or close-fitting skirts, accompanied by a form-fitting bodice. The skirt is often ankle length and sometimes has a slit in either the front, side, or back to make walking easier.

Shelf bra - A bra that is built right into the garment.

Shirred waist - A decorative gathering (as of cloth) made by drawing up the material along two or more parallel lines of stitching.

Shrug - A woman's small, waist-length or shorter jacket.

Skant - Pants that have a sweater-like attachment around the waist.

Skort - Shorts that have a front covering to resemble a skirt.

Spaghetti strap - A thin tubular strap that attaches to the bodice, named for its likeness to a strand of spaghetti.

Split neck - A round neckline that looks like it has been cut in the center to form a small "V".

Square neck - An open-yoke neckline shaped in the form of a half square.

Straight legs - Pant legs are cut an equal width from waist to ankle.

Sweep train - The shortest train, barely sweeping the floor.
Sweetheart neck - A graceful, open yoke, shaped like the top half of a heart.

Tank top - A short sleeveless top with wide armholes.

Tankini - two piece bathing suit with the upper portion resembling a tank top.

Tapered legs - Pant legs become progressively narrower toward the ankle.

Tea length - A gown hemmed to end at the shin.

Tear-away shorts - Features versatile side snaps that allow you to remove a top layer fast.

Tie-cinched waist - The waist is pulled tight around the body with a tie.

Trapeze top - Tank top style with flared bottom.

Tulle skirt/bouffant gown - A sheer, puffed-out skirt often made of stiffened silk, rayon, or nylon net.

Tunic style - A simple slip-on garment made with or without sleeves and usually knee-length or longer, belted at the waist, and worn as an under or outer garment.

Turtle neck - A high, close-fitting, turnover collar used especially for sweaters.

V-neck/V-back - An open yoke coming to a "V" shape midway down the bodice.

Variegated - Having streaks, marks, or patches of different colors; distinguished or characterized by a variety of different colors.

Wedding-band collar - A collar featuring a yoke that is either open or of sheer net with an ornate band fitting snugly on the neck, creating a choker effect.

Wide legs - Pants or jeans that are cut extra full through the legs.

Wing collar - A collar with projections which cover shoulder seams of bodices and doublets.

Wrap top/surplice top - A bodice created by the cross-wrapping of fabric; may be in front or back, and associated with a high or low neckline

ABOUT THE AUTHOR

It has been said that a person should look as if they bought their clothes with intelligence, put them on with care, and then forget all about them. With this intricacy and intent, Cedric S. King has mastered the art of being a well-dressed man, who dresses others with the same intent.

After establishing adoration for all things fashionable from lifestyle to wardrobe and engaging in a fulfilling retail career, King took a three-year sabbatical in Italy. During this extended jaunt, the fashion expert set up shop in Northern Italy and indulged himself in the art of male fashion with an emphasis on men's suiting and dress shirts and accessories including neckties, bowties, ascots and scarves. From this studying, he realized that introducing a concept of combining two polar opposites in the fashion spectrum – "Preppy" and "Rugged" would make a strong impact on the burgeoning American hip-hop culture. Instantaneously, King successfully combined dapper elements of quality, style and comfort with the strong flavor of the streets, giving birth to the Dap-Rugget brand.

Spreading the gospel of a second coming of gingham, plaid and paisley from 1999 to 2009, Cedric established his name in the fashion industry by shipping to over 500 specialty boutiques and establishing a loyal customer base. Because he understood the connection between fashion and music, King utilized his relationships with well-known industry professionals, artists and personalities including Jay-Z, Outkast, T.I., Jagged Edge, A Tribe Called Quest, Goodie Mob, Usher, Rockmond Dunbar and Musiq Soulchild to create brand awareness.

With the high regard he garnered as a force in fashion, Cedric decided to broaden the scope of his business dealings and opened DR Design Studios, a full-service product development and design company.

Because of the precedence of his reputation, some major clients included: Russell Corporation, Discus Brand, Hobie, Goody's Family Clothing, AKOO, Rocawear, RyanKenny, Sean John and Oxford Industries. As a strategic alliance, Cedric accepted a position as Vice President of Product Development and Design with The Romar Group Inc., the nation's largest minority owned and operated clothing manufacturer, #38 in Black Enterprise in 2004 with reported annual sells of 90 million dollars. King states, "As a designer, I have always understood that if I delivered a quality product and designed it from the inside out, it could always be worn no matter how much time passes or what trends emerge."

Now, after giving a pulse to over 100 fashion brands, King bides his time between philanthropy and education in the name of all things stylish. In his interaction with up-and-coming designers, tastemakers and trendsetters, he is gearing up for a new coming. He explains, "The social uniform era is over and the PUSH era has begun. "PUSH", a personification of Preppy, Urban, Street and Hipster style, is creating an influential lifestyle brand that supports true personal style." PUSH AESTHETICS CLOTHING was released in the fall of 2016 in tribute to the current forecast of individual living. "We are in a time where being an individual is more important than fitting in, which allows us to create capsule collections that are colorful, socially simulating, directional, innovative, and risky," he continues.

Cedric currently resides in Atlanta where he wears many hats as an author (Prep 101, "The Battle of Status and Social Rank"), designer (DAP-RUGGET, PUSH AESTHETICS CLOTHING, Andover & Hotchkiss) and fashion entrepreneur. "Today I think people are designing based on what they think people want, and I think it is my job as a great designer/innovator to give people what they don't know they want yet, "he declares. The best is yet to come.

FOR MORINFORMATION VISIT
WWW.THEFASHIONHUSTLE.COM